I0426144

Evaluation of the Sensitivity of Inventory and Monitoring National Parks to Acidification Effects from Atmospheric Sulfur and Nitrogen Deposition

Upper Columbia Basin Network (UCBN)

Natural Resource Report NPS/NRPC/ARD/NRR—2011/382

T. J. Sullivan
T. C. McDonnell
G. T. McPherson
S. D. Mackey
D. Moore

E&S Environmental Chemistry, Inc.
P.O. Box 609
Corvallis, OR 97339

April 2011

U.S. Department of the Interior
National Park Service
Natural Resource Program Center
Denver, Colorado

The National Park Service, Natural Resource Program Center publishes a range of reports that address natural resource topics of interest and applicability to a broad audience in the National Park Service and others in natural resource management, including scientists, conservation and environmental constituencies, and the public.

The Natural Resource Report Series is used to disseminate high-priority, current natural resource management information with managerial application. The series targets a general, diverse audience, and may contain NPS policy considerations or address sensitive issues of management applicability.

All manuscripts in the series receive the appropriate level of peer review to ensure that the information is scientifically credible, technically accurate, appropriately written for the intended audience, and designed and published in a professional manner.

This report received peer review by subject-matter experts who were not directly involved in the collection, analysis, or reporting of the data. Data in this report were collected and analyzed using methods based on established, peer-reviewed protocols and were analyzed and interpreted within the guidelines of the protocols.

Views, statements, findings, conclusions, recommendations, and data in this report do not necessarily reflect views and policies of the National Park Service, U.S. Department of the Interior. Mention of trade names or commercial products does not constitute endorsement or recommendation for use by the U.S. Government.

This report is available from Air Resources Division of the NPS (http://www.nature.nps.gov/air/Permits/ARIS/networks/acidification-eval.cfm) and the Natural Resource Publications Management website (http://www.nature.nps.gov/publications/nrpm/).

Please cite this publication as:

Sullivan, T. J., G. T. McPherson, T. C. McDonnell, S. D. Mackey, and D. Moore. 2011. Evaluation of the sensitivity of inventory and monitoring national parks to acidification effects from atmospheric sulfur and nitrogen deposition: Upper Columbia Basin Network (UCBN). Natural Resource Report NPS/NRPC/ARD/NRR—2011/382. National Park Service, Denver, Colorado.

NPS 963/107420, April 2011

Upper Columbia Basin Network (UCBN)

National maps of atmospheric S and N emissions and deposition are provided in Maps A through D as context for subsequent network data presentations. Maps A and B show county level emissions of total S and total N for the year 2002. Maps C and D show total S and total N deposition, again for the year 2002.

There are eight parks in the Upper Columbia Basin Network. Two of them are larger than 100 square miles: Craters of the Moon (CRMO) and Lake Roosevelt (LARO).

Total annual S and N emissions, by county, are shown in Maps E and F, respectively, for lands in and surrounding the Upper Columbia Basin Network. County level S emissions were generally low, mostly less than 1 ton per square mile, with a few small areas having emissions between 1 and 5 tons per square mile. County-level annual N emissions within the network were somewhat higher, generally ranging from less than 1 ton per square mile to more than 5 tons per square mile. There were a few small areas in Idaho where N emissions were between 5 and 20 tons per square mile. There were few point source emissions of SO_2 in the network, and they were relatively small: all but one emitted less than 5,000 tons S per year (Map G). Point source emissions of oxidized (nitrogen oxides, NO_x) and reduced (ammonia, NH_3) N are shown in Map H. There were few N point sources of any magnitude in this network.

Urban centers within the network and within a 300-mile buffer around the network are shown in Map I. There are only two population centers larger than 100,000 and none larger than 500,000 within the network. There are several large urban centers within the 300-mile buffer, including Seattle, Portland, San Francisco, and San Jose.

Total S and N deposition in and around the network are shown in Maps J and K, respectively. Included in this analysis are both wet and dry forms of deposition and both the oxidized and reduced N species. Total S deposition is low throughout the entire network, less than 2 kg S/ha/yr. Total N deposition within most of the network ranged from less than 2 kg N/ha/yr to 2 to 5 kg N/ha/yr, with pockets of estimated deposition higher than that.

Land cover in and around the network is shown in Map L. The predominant cover types within this network are generally quite varied. They include mainly forest and row crops in the north, and shrubland and grassland/herbaceous in the south.

Land slope within parks that occur in this network is shown in Map M. Park land slope is less than 10° in CRMO and between 10° and 20° in LARO. Average slope is steeper, between 20° and 30°, in all of the smaller parks except Whitman Mission (WHMI), where slope is less than 10°.

Park lands requiring special protection against potential adverse impacts associated with acidic deposition are shown on Map N. Also shown on Map N are all federal lands designated as wilderness, both lands managed by NPS and lands managed by other federal agencies. The land designations used to identify this heightened protection included Class I designation under the Clean Air Act Amendments and wilderness designation. The only Class I or wilderness area managed by NPS in this network is a small area in CRMO. There is, however, substantial wilderness outside NPS jurisdiction.

Network rankings are given in Figures A through C as the average ranking of the Pollutant Exposure, Ecosystem Sensitivity, and Park Protection metrics, respectively. Figure D shows the overall network Summary Risk ranking. In each figure, the rank for this particular network is highlighted to show its relative position compared with the ranks of the other 31 networks.

The Upper Columbia Basin Network ranked in the lowest quintile among networks in S and N-Pollutant Exposure (Figure A). Emissions and deposition of both S and N within the network are low. The network Ecosystem Sensitivity ranking was the lowest of all networks (Figure B). This is because the network is not located in an area of known acid sensitivity, there is no vegetation coverage in the I&M parks that includes vegetation types expected to be especially sensitive to acidic deposition, and there are no high-elevation lakes and few low-order, high-elevation streams. This network ranked in the second lowest quintile in Park Protection, having limited amounts of protected lands (Figure C).

In combination, the network rankings for Pollutant Exposure, Ecosystem Sensitivity, and Park Protection yielded an overall Network Risk ranking that is the lowest of all networks (Figure D). The overall level of concern for acidification effects on I&M parks within this network is considered Very Low.

Similarly, park rankings are given in Figures E through H for the same metrics. In the case of the park rankings, we only show in the figures the parks that are larger than 100 square miles. Relative ranks for all parks, including the smaller parks, are given in Table A and Appendix A. As for the network rankings, the park rankings highlight those parks that occur in this network to show their relative position compared with parks in the other 31 networks. Note that the rankings shown in Figures E through H reflect the rank of a given park compared with all other parks, irrespective of size.

Two of the parks in the Upper Columbia Basin Network were ranked in the second lowest quintile for Pollutant Exposure: Hagerman Fossil Beds (HAFO) and WHMI; neither is large. The other parks in the network were ranked in the lowest quintile for this theme (Table A, Figure E). Ecosystem Sensitivity rankings varied, with CRMO and WHMI ranked in the lowest quintile, and City of Rocks (CIRO) ranked in the second highest. The other five parks were ranked in the middle quintile for Ecosystem Sensitivity (Moderate risk). All of the parks except CRMO were ranked in the middle quintile for Park Protection; CRMO was ranked High, in the second highest quintile.

The Summary Risk ranked two small parks as Moderate. Other parks, including both of the larger parks (CRMO and LARO), were ranked Low for overall risk of acidification effects.

Table A. Relative rankings of individual I&M parks within the network for Pollutant Exposure, Ecosystem Sensitivity, Park Protection, and overall Summary Risk from acidic deposition.

I&M Parks[2] in Network	Relative Ranking of Individual Parks[1]			
	Pollutant Exposure	Ecosystem Sensitivity	Park Protection	Summary Risk
Big Hole	Very Low	Moderate	Moderate	Low
City of Rocks	Very Low	High	Moderate	Moderate
Craters of the Moon	Very Low	Very Low	High	Low
Hagerman Fossil Beds	Low	Moderate	Moderate	Moderate
John Day Fossil Beds	Very Low	Moderate	Moderate	Low
Lake Roosevelt	Very Low	Moderate	Moderate	Low
Nez Perce	Very Low	Moderate	Moderate	Low
Whitman Mission	Low	Very Low	Moderate	Low

[1] Relative park rankings are designated according to quintile ranking, among all I&M Parks, from the lowest quintile (very low risk) to the highest quintile (very high risk).

[2] Park name is printed in bold italic for parks larger than 100 square miles.

Map A. National map of total S emissions by county for the year 2002, in units of tons of S per square mile per year. (Source of data: EPA National Emissions Inventory, http://www.epa.gov/ttn/chief/net/2002inventory.html)

Map B. National map of total N emissions by county for the year 2002. Both oxidized (nitrogen oxides, NO_x) and reduced (ammonia, NH_3) forms of N are included. The total is expressed in tons per square mile per year. (Source of data: EPA National Emissions Inventory, http://www.epa.gov/ttn/chief/net/2002inventory.html)

Map C. Total S deposition for the conterminous United States for the year 2002, expressed in units of kilograms of S deposited from the atmosphere to the Earth surface per hectare per year. For the eastern half of the country, wet deposition values were derived from interpolated measured values from NADP (three-year average centered on 2002) and dry deposition values were derived from 12-km CMAQ model projections for 2002. For the western half of the country, both wet and dry deposition values were derived from 36-km CMAQ model projections for 2002. NADP interpolations were performed using the approach of Grimm and Lynch (1997). CMAQ model projections were provided by Robin Dennis, U.S. EPA.

Map D. Total N deposition for the conterminous United States for the year 2002, expressed in units of kilograms of N deposited from the atmosphere to the Earth surface per hectare per year. Wet and dry forms of both oxidized (nitrogen oxides, NO_x) and reduced (ammonia, NH_3) N are included. For the eastern half of the country, wet deposition values were derived from interpolated measured values from NADP (three-year average centered on 2002) and dry deposition values were derived from 12-km CMAQ model projections for 2002. For the western half of the country, both wet and dry deposition values were derived from 36-km CMAQ model projections for 2002. NADP interpolations were performed using the approach of Grimm and Lynch (1997). CMAQ model projections were provided by Robin Dennis, U.S. EPA.

Map E.   Total S emissions by county for lands surrounding the network, expressed as tons of S emitted into the atmosphere per square mile per year. (Source of data: EPA National Emissions Inventory, http://www.epa.gov/ttn/chief/net/2002inventory.html)

Map F.   Total N emissions by county for lands surrounding the network, expressed as tons of N emitted into the atmosphere per square mile per year. The total includes both oxidized (nitrogen oxides, NO_x) and reduced (ammonia, NH_3) N. (Source of data: EPA National Emissions Inventory, http://www.epa.gov/ttn/chief/net/ 2002inventory.html)

Map G.   Major point source emissions of SO_2 for lands surrounding the network. (Source of data: EPA National Emissions Inventory, http://www.epa.gov/ttn/chief/net/ 2002inventory.html)

Map H.   Major point source emissions of oxidized (nitrogen oxides, NO_x) and reduced (ammonia, NH_3) N in and around the network. The base of each vertical bar is positioned in the map at the approximate location of the source. The height of the bar is proportional to the magnitude of the source. (Source of data: EPA National Emissions Inventory, http://www.epa.gov/ttn/chief/net/2002inventory.html)

Map I.   Urban centers having more than 10,000 people within the network and within a 300-mile buffer around the perimeter of the network. (Source of data: U.S. Census 2000)

Map J.   Total S deposition in and around the network. Values are expressed as kilograms of S deposited per hectare per year. (Source of data: Interpolated NADP wet and CMAQ Model dry deposition data for 2002; see information for Map C above for details)

Map K.   Total N deposition in and around the network. Included in the total are wet plus dry forms of both oxidized (nitrogen oxides, NO_x) and reduced (ammonia, NH_3) N. Values are expressed as kilograms of N deposited per hectare per year. (Source of data: Interpolated NADP wet and CMAQ Model dry deposition data for 2002; see information for Map D above for details)

Map L.   Land cover types in and around the network, based on the National Land Cover dataset. (Source of data: National Land Cover Dataset, http://www.mrlc.gov/nlcd_multizone_map.php)

Map M.   Average land slope within park units that occur within the network, by 10-digit HUC. Some parks in this network are slightly larger than 100 mi^2, but yet too small to readily see the color within the park outline. These parks are represented on the map with a colored circle and a line from the circle indicating the park location. (Source of data: U.S. EPA National Elevation Dataset [http://ned.usgs.gov/])

Map N. Lands within the network that are classified as Class I or wilderness area. (Source of data: USGS 2005 [National Atlas; http://nationalatlas.gov] and NPS)

Figure A. Network rankings for Pollutant Exposure, calculated as the average of scores for all Pollutant Exposure variables.

Figure B. Network rankings for Ecosystem Sensitivity, calculated as the average of scores for all Ecosystem Sensitivity variables.

Figure C. Network rankings for Park Protection, calculated as the average of scores for all Park Protection variables.

Figure D. Summary Network Risk Ranking, calculated as the average of the quintile ranks for the Pollutant Exposure, Ecosystem Sensitivity, and Park Protection themes.

Figure E. Park rankings for Pollutant Exposure for all parks larger than 100 square miles. Ranks for each park were calculated relative to all parks, regardless of size, as the average of scores for all Pollutant Exposure variables.

Figure F. Park rankings for Ecosystem Sensitivity for all parks larger than 100 square miles. Ranks for each park were calculated relative to all parks, regardless of size, as the average of scores for all Ecosystem Sensitivity variables.

Figure G. Park rankings for Park Protection for all parks larger than 100 square miles. Ranks for each park were calculated relative to all parks, regardless of size, as the average of scores for all Park Protection variables.

Figure H. Park rankings for Summary Risk for all parks larger than 100 square miles. Ranks for each park were calculated relative to all parks, regardless of size, as the average of the quintile ranks for the Pollutant Exposure, Ecosystem Sensitivity, and Park Protection themes.

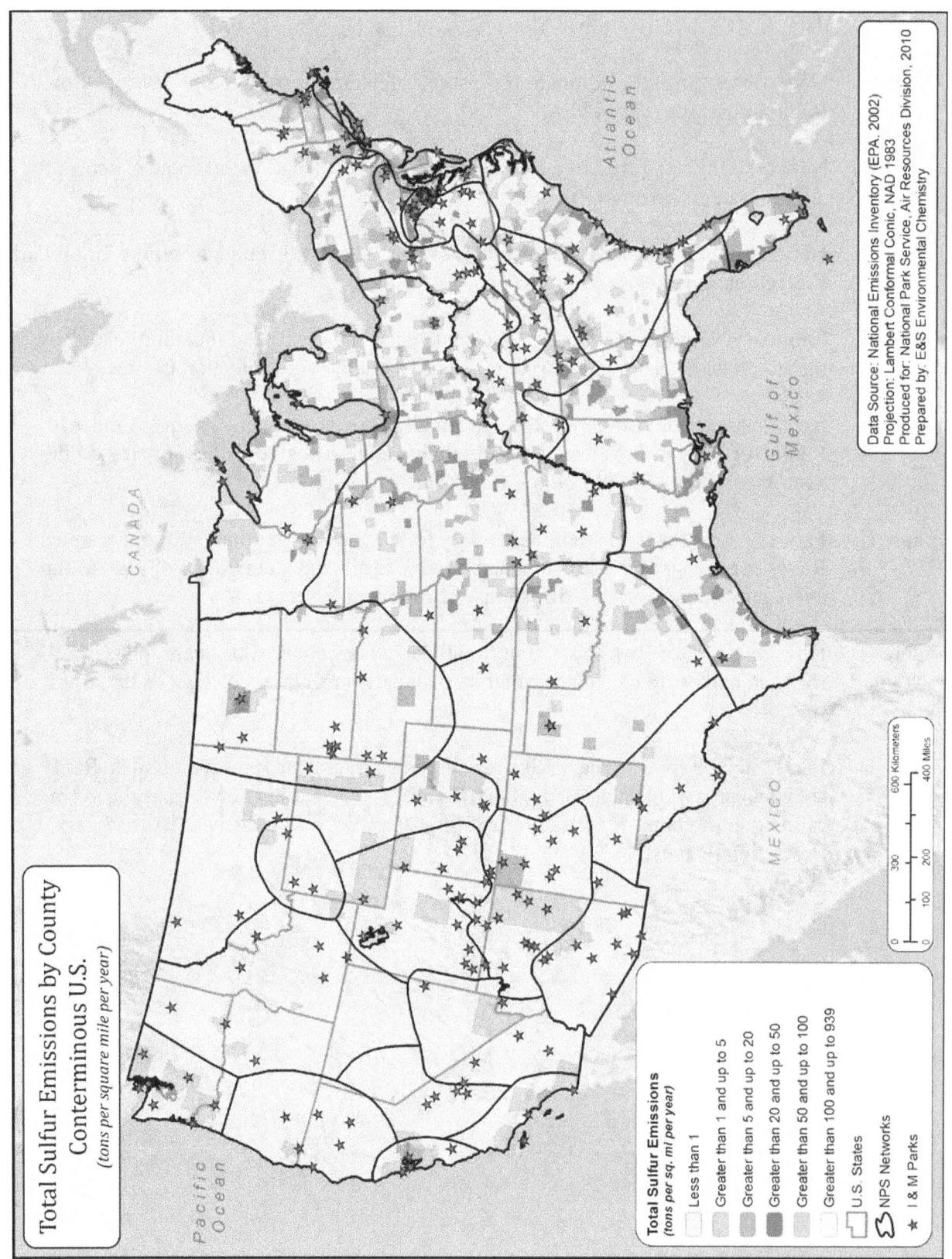

Total Sulfur Emissions by County Conterminous U.S.
(tons per square mile per year)

Total Sulfur Emissions
(tons per sq. mi per year)

- Less than 1
- Greater than 1 and up to 5
- Greater than 5 and up to 20
- Greater than 20 and up to 50
- Greater than 50 and up to 100
- Greater than 100 and up to 939
- U.S. States
- NPS Networks
- I & M Parks

Data Source: National Emissions Inventory (EPA, 2002)
Projection: Lambert Conformal Conic, NAD 1983
Produced for: National Park Service, Air Resources Division, 2010
Prepared by: E&S Environmental Chemistry

Map A

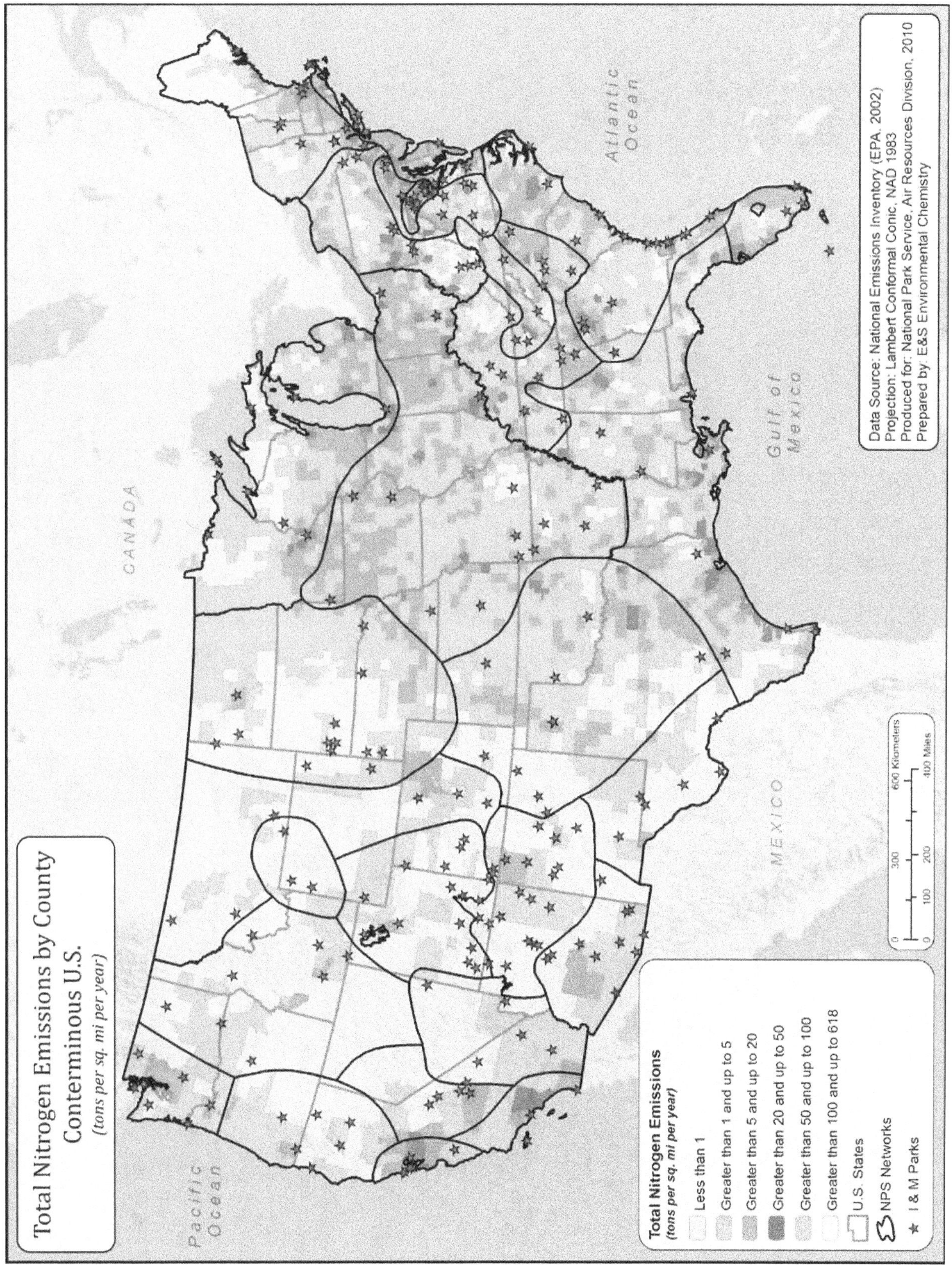

Total Nitrogen Emissions by County
Conterminous U.S.
(tons per sq. mi per year)
Pacific Ocean
CANADA
Atlantic Ocean
Gulf of Mexico
MEXICO
Total Nitrogen Emissions
(tons per sq. mi per year)
Less than 1
Greater than 1 and up to 5
Greater than 5 and up to 20
Greater than 20 and up to 50
Greater than 50 and up to 100
Greater than 100 and up to 618
U.S. States
NPS Networks
I & M Parks
0 300 600 Kilometers
0 100 200 400 Miles
Data Source: National Emissions Inventory (EPA, 2002)
Projection: Lambert Conformal Conic, NAD 1983
Produced for: National Park Service, Air Resources Division, 2010
Prepared by: E&S Environmental Chemistry

Map B

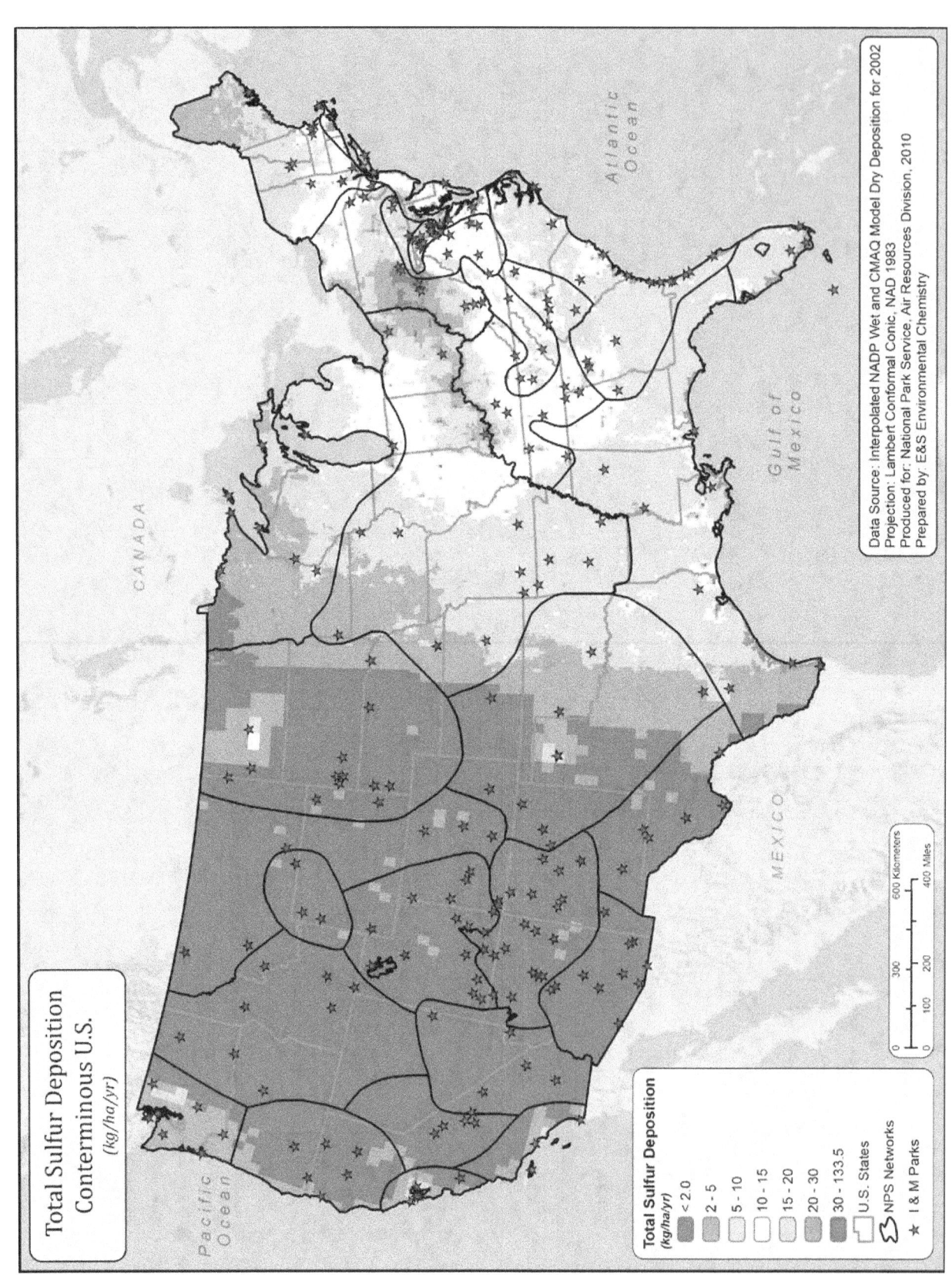

Total Sulfur Deposition Conterminous U.S.
(kg/ha/yr)

Total Sulfur Deposition
(kg/ha/yr)

< 2.0
2 - 5
5 - 10
10 - 15
15 - 20
20 - 30
30 - 133.5

U.S. States
NPS Networks
I & M Parks

Data Source: Interpolated NADP Wet and CMAQ Model Dry Deposition for 2002
Projection: Lambert Conformal Conic, NAD 1983
Produced for: National Park Service, Air Resources Division, 2010
Prepared by: E&S Environmental Chemistry

Map C

Total Nitrogen Deposition Conterminous U.S.
(kg/ha/yr)

Total Nitrogen Deposition
(kg/ha/yr)

- < 2.0
- 2 - 5
- 5 - 10
- 10 - 15
- 15 - 20
- 20 - 30
- 30 - 63.5

U.S. States

NPS Networks

I & M Parks

Pacific Ocean

Atlantic Ocean

Gulf of Mexico

CANADA

MEXICO

Data Source: Interpolated NADP Wet and CMAQ Model Dry Deposition for 2002
Projection: Lambert Conformal Conic, NAD 1983
Produced for: National Park Service, Air Resources Division, 2010
Prepared by: E&S Environmental Chemistry

0   100   200   300   400 Miles
0   300   600 Kilometers

Map D

Total Sulfur Emissions by County
Upper Columbia Basin Network
(tons per square mile per year)

Locator Map

Total S Emissions *(tons per sq. mi per year)*

Less than 1
Greater than 1 and up to 5
Greater than 5 and up to 20
Greater than 20 and up to 50
Greater than 50 and up to 100
Greater than 100 and up to 939

U.S. States
Upper Columbia Basin Network
Network Parks (larger than 100 sq. mi)
Network Parks (smaller than 100 sq. mi)

100 Kilometers
100 Miles

CANADA

Pacific Ocean

Data Source: National Emissions Inventory (EPA, 2002)
Projection: Lambert Conformal Conic, NAD 1983
Produced for: National Park Service, Air Resources Division. 2010
Prepared by: E&S Environmental Chemistry

Map E

UCBN-10

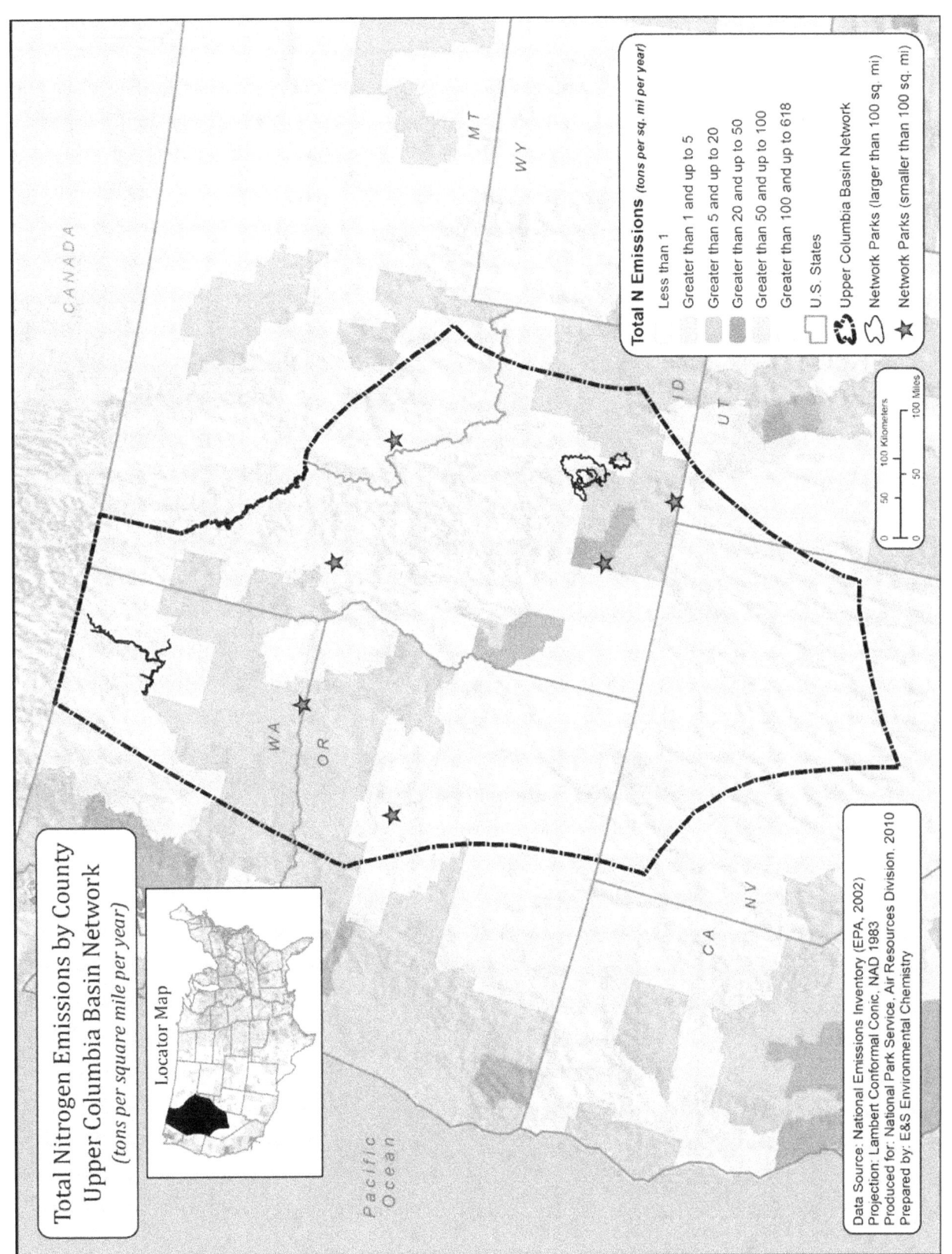

Total Nitrogen Emissions by County
Upper Columbia Basin Network
(tons per square mile per year)

Locator Map

Total N Emissions *(tons per sq. mi per year)*

Less than 1
Greater than 1 and up to 5
Greater than 5 and up to 20
Greater than 20 and up to 50
Greater than 50 and up to 100
Greater than 100 and up to 618

U.S. States
Upper Columbia Basin Network
Network Parks (larger than 100 sq. mi)
Network Parks (smaller than 100 sq. mi)

CANADA

M T
W Y
I D
U T
W A
O R
N V
C A

Pacific Ocean

0   50   100 Kilometers
0   50   100 Miles

Data Source: National Emissions Inventory (EPA, 2002)
Projection: Lambert Conformal Conic, NAD 1983
Produced for: National Park Service, Air Resources Division, 2010
Prepared by: E&S Environmental Chemistry

Map F

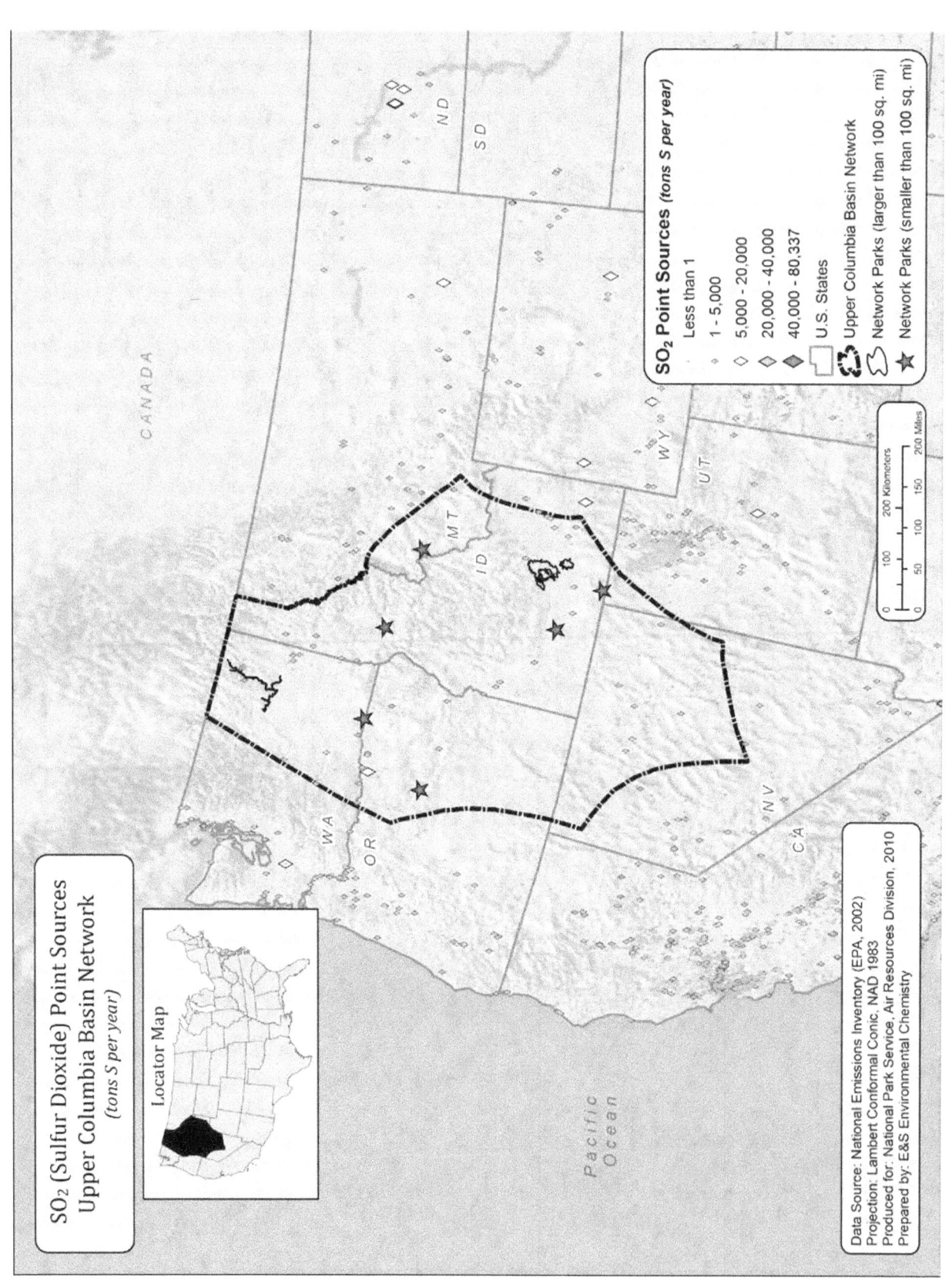

SO₂ (Sulfur Dioxide) Point Sources
Upper Columbia Basin Network
(tons S per year)

Locator Map

SO₂ Point Sources *(tons S per year)*

Less than 1
1 - 5,000
5,000 - 20,000
20,000 - 40,000
40,000 - 80,337
U.S. States
Upper Columbia Basin Network
Network Parks (larger than 100 sq. mi)
Network Parks (smaller than 100 sq. mi)

CANADA

ND
SD
MT
ID
WY
UT
WA
OR
NV
CA

Pacific Ocean

0 100 200 Kilometers
0 50 100 150 200 Miles

Data Source: National Emissions Inventory (EPA, 2002)
Projection: Lambert Conformal Conic, NAD 1983
Produced for: National Park Service, Air Resources Division, 2010
Prepared by: E&S Environmental Chemistry

Map G

UCBN-12

NOₓ (Nitrogen Oxides) and NH₃
(Ammonia) Point Sources
Upper Columbia Basin Network
(tons N per year)

Locator Map

NOₓ Point Sources *(tons N per year)*

2,500 tons N/year

NH₃ Point Sources *(tons N per year)*

1,000 tons N/year

U.S. States

Upper Columbia Basin Network

Network Parks (larger than 100 sq. mi)

Network Parks (smaller than 100 sq. mi)

CANADA

ND
SD
MT
ID
WY
UT
NV
CA
WA
OR

Pacific
Ocean

0   50   100   150   200 Miles
0   100   200 Kilometers

Data Source: National Emissions Inventory (EPA, 2002)
Projection: Lambert Conformal Conic, NAD 1983
Produced for: National Park Service, Air Resources Division, 2010
Prepared by: E&S Environmental Chemistry

Map H

UCBN-13

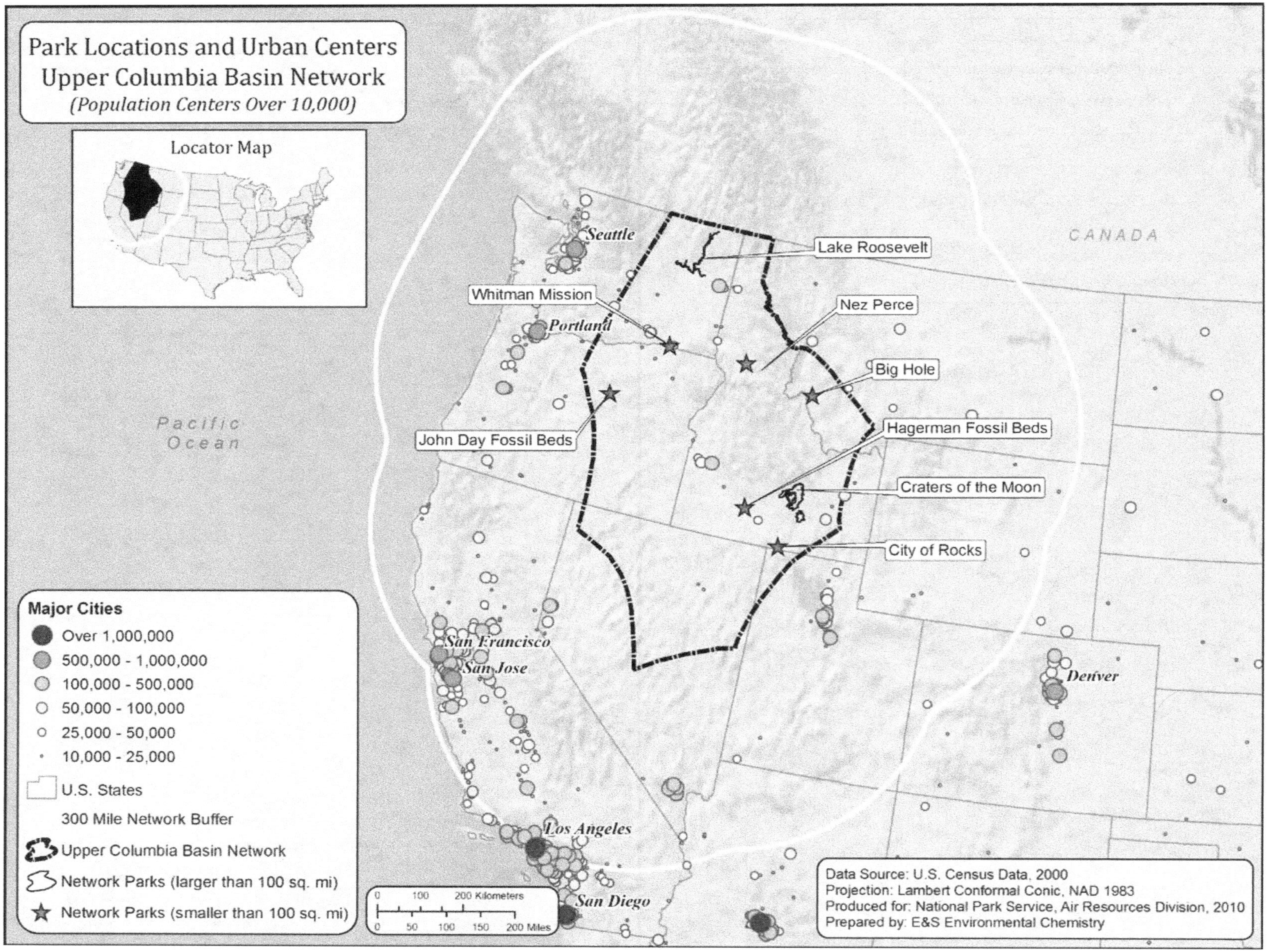

Park Locations and Urban Centers
Upper Columbia Basin Network
(Population Centers Over 10,000)

Locator Map

CANADA

Denver

Lake Roosevelt
Nez Perce
Big Hole
Hagerman Fossil Beds
Craters of the Moon
City of Rocks

Seattle
Whitman Mission
Portland
John Day Fossil Beds

San Francisco
San Jose
Los Angeles
San Diego

Pacific Ocean

Major Cities
- Over 1,000,000
- 500,000 - 1,000,000
- 100,000 - 500,000
- 50,000 - 100,000
- 25,000 - 50,000
- 10,000 - 25,000

U.S. States

300 Mile Network Buffer

Upper Columbia Basin Network

Network Parks (larger than 100 sq. mi)

★ Network Parks (smaller than 100 sq. mi)

0   100   200 Kilometers
0   50   100   150   200 Miles

Data Source: U.S. Census Data, 2000
Projection: Lambert Conformal Conic, NAD 1983
Produced for: National Park Service, Air Resources Division, 2010
Prepared by: E&S Environmental Chemistry

Map I

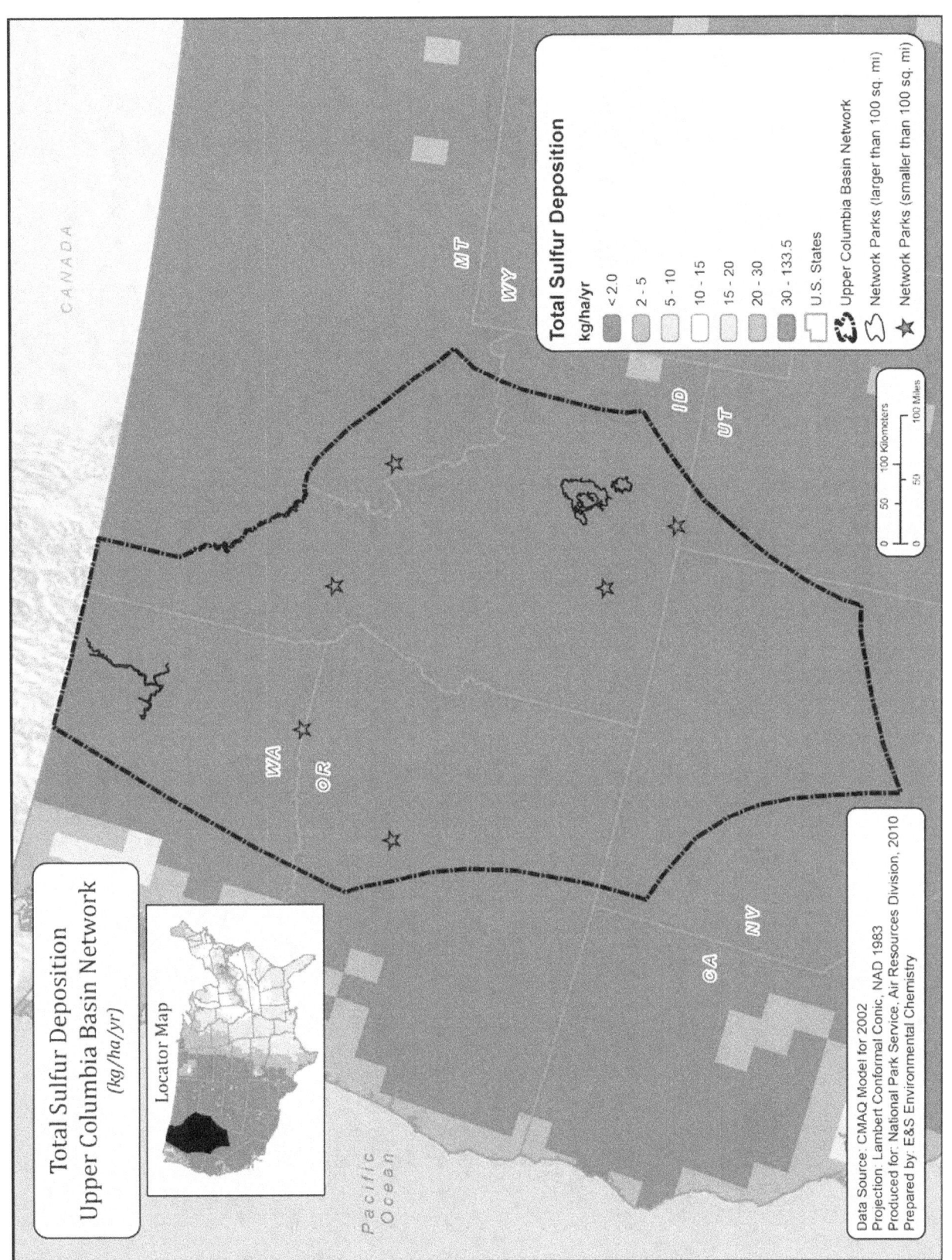

Total Sulfur Deposition
Upper Columbia Basin Network
(kg/ha/yr)

Locator Map

Pacific Ocean

CANADA

WA

OR

MT

WY

ID

UT

CA

NV

Total Sulfur Deposition

kg/ha/yr

- < 2.0
- 2 - 5
- 5 - 10
- 10 - 15
- 15 - 20
- 20 - 30
- 30 - 133.5
- U.S. States

Upper Columbia Basin Network

★ Network Parks (larger than 100 sq. mi)

★ Network Parks (smaller than 100 sq. mi)

0   50   100 Kilometers
0   50   100 Miles

Data Source: CMAQ Model for 2002
Projection: Lambert Conformal Conic, NAD 1983
Produced for: National Park Service, Air Resources Division, 2010
Prepared by: E&S Environmental Chemistry

Map J

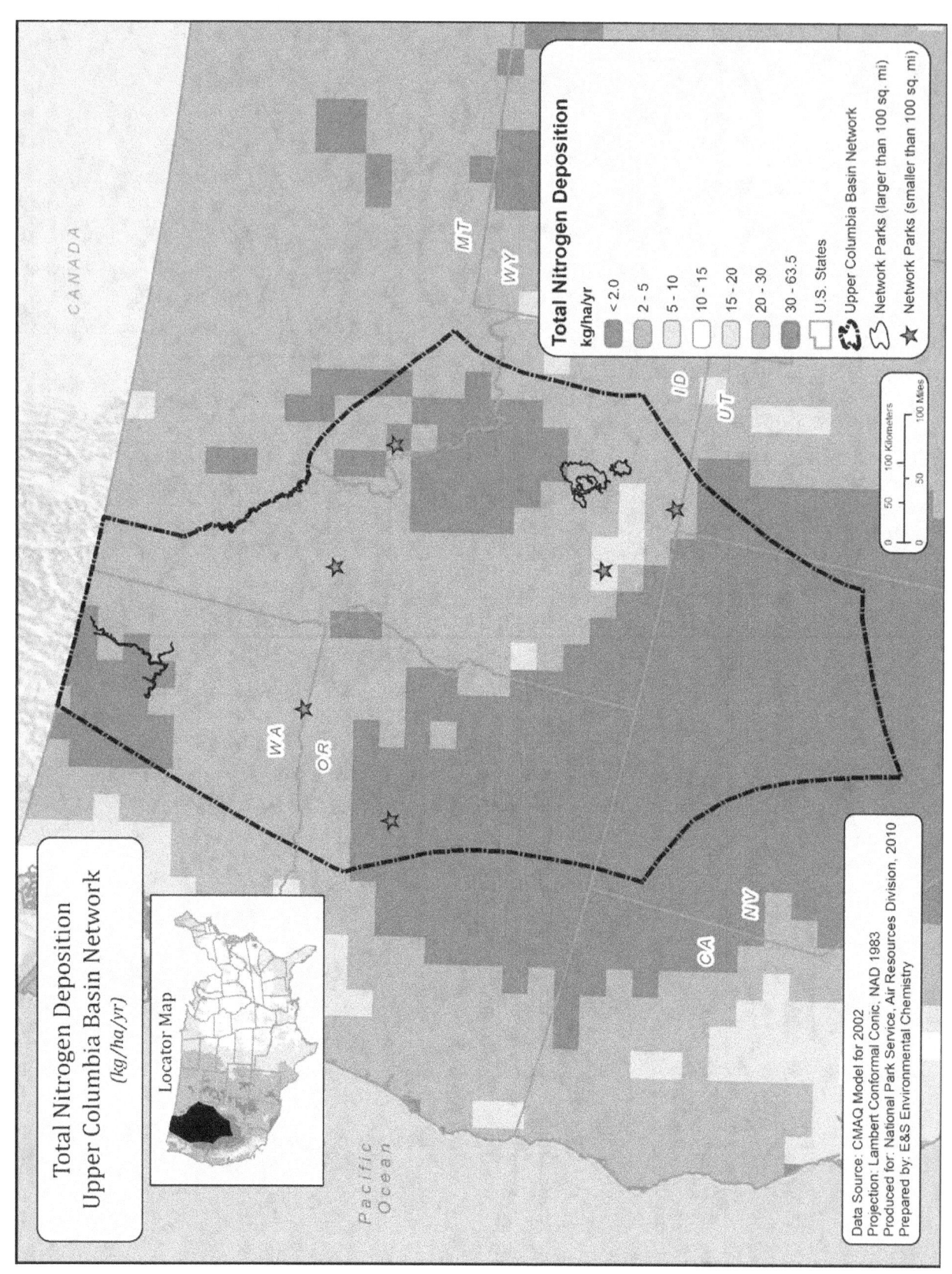

Total Nitrogen Deposition
Upper Columbia Basin Network
(kg/ha/yr)

Locator Map

Total Nitrogen Deposition

kg/ha/yr
- < 2.0
- 2 - 5
- 5 - 10
- 10 - 15
- 15 - 20
- 20 - 30
- 30 - 63.5
- U.S. States
- Upper Columbia Basin Network
- Network Parks (larger than 100 sq. mi)
- Network Parks (smaller than 100 sq. mi)

CANADA

Pacific Ocean

MT
WY
ID
UT
WA
OR
CA
NV

Data Source: CMAQ Model for 2002
Projection: Lambert Conformal Conic, NAD 1983
Produced for: National Park Service, Air Resources Division, 2010
Prepared by: E&S Environmental Chemistry

0   50   100 Kilometers
0   50   100 Miles

Map K

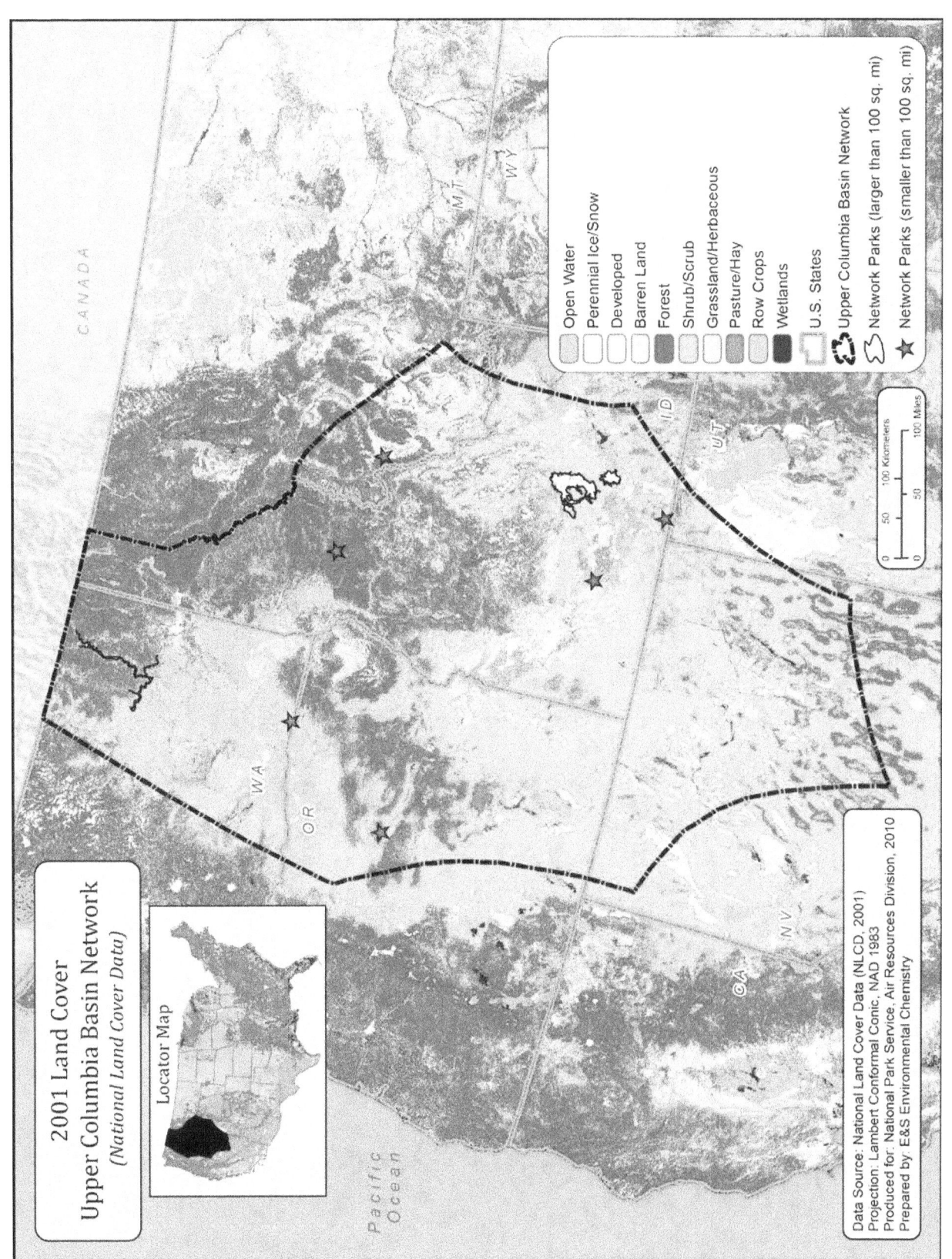

2001 Land Cover
Upper Columbia Basin Network
(National Land Cover Data)

Locator Map

Legend:
- Open Water
- Perennial Ice/Snow
- Developed
- Barren Land
- Forest
- Shrub/Scrub
- Grassland/Herbaceous
- Pasture/Hay
- Row Crops
- Wetlands
- U.S. States
- Upper Columbia Basin Network
- Network Parks (larger than 100 sq. mi)
- Network Parks (smaller than 100 sq. mi)

CANADA

MT
WY
ID
UT
WA
OR
NV
CA

Pacific Ocean

100 Kilometers
100 Miles
0   50
0   50

Data Source: National Land Cover Data (NLCD, 2001)
Projection: Lambert Conformal Conic, NAD 1983
Produced for: National Park Service, Air Resources Division, 2010
Prepared by: E&S Environmental Chemistry

Map L

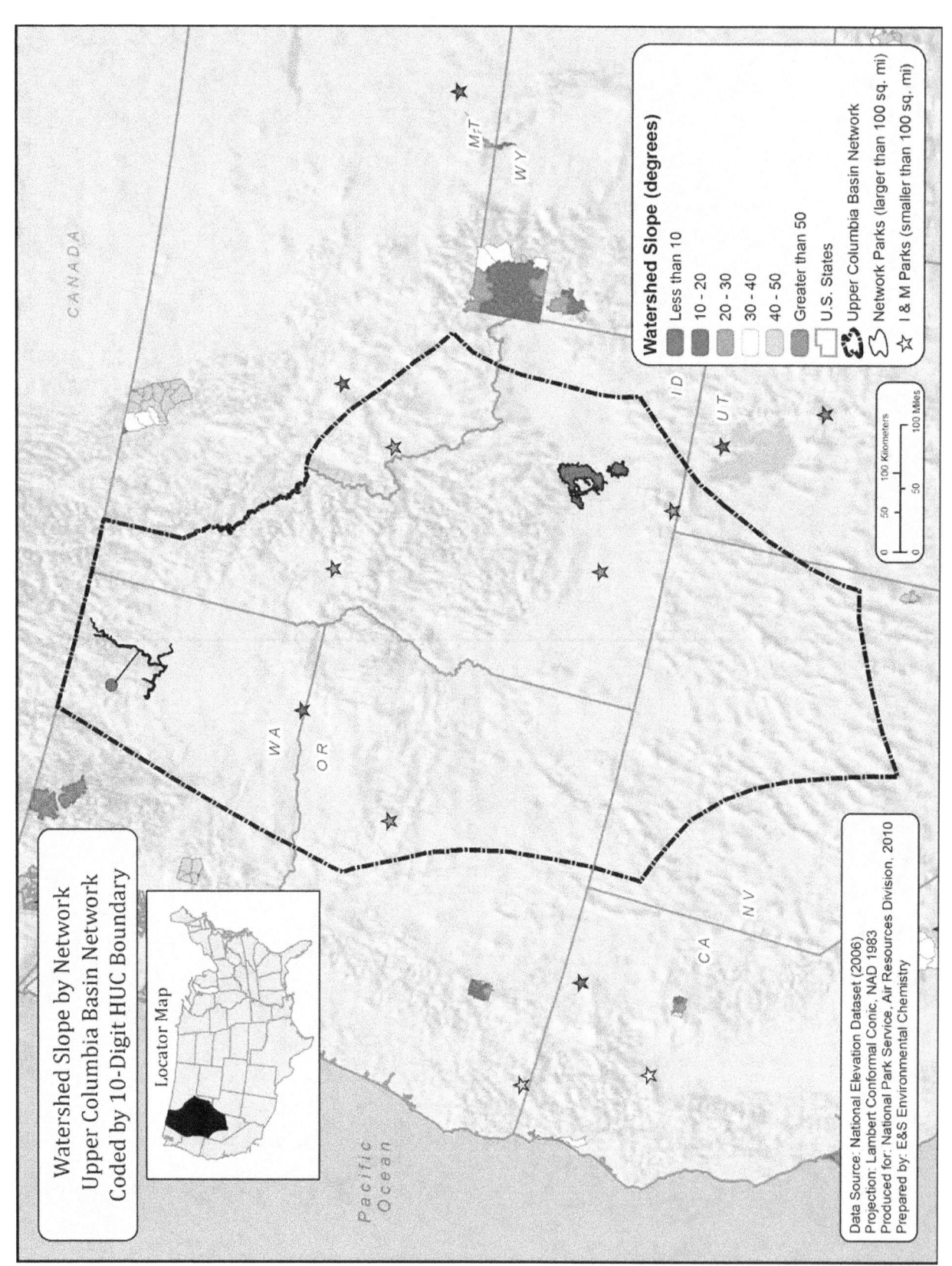

Watershed Slope by Network
Upper Columbia Basin Network
Coded by 10-Digit HUC Boundary

Locator Map

Watershed Slope (degrees)

Less than 10
10 - 20
20 - 30
30 - 40
40 - 50
Greater than 50
U.S. States
Upper Columbia Basin Network
Network Parks (larger than 100 sq. mi)
I & M Parks (smaller than 100 sq. mi)

CANADA

Pacific Ocean

M T
W Y
I D
U T
W A
O R
N V
C A

Data Source: National Elevation Dataset (2006)
Projection: Lambert Conformal Conic, NAD 1983
Produced for: National Park Service, Air Resources Division, 2010
Prepared by: E&S Environmental Chemistry

Map M

UCBN-18

Class I and Wilderness Areas
Upper Columbia Basin Network

Locator Map

Class I and Wilderness Areas

Wilderness
NPS Class I
NPS Class I and Wilderness Overlap
U.S. States
Upper Columbia Basin Network
Network Parks (larger than 100 sq. mi)
Network Parks (smaller than 100 sq. mi)

CANADA

MT

WY

ID

UT

WA

OR

NV

CA

Pacific Ocean

50   100 Kilometers
50   100 Miles

Data Source: National Park Service (2007) and National Atlas (2005)
Projection: Lambert Conformal Conic, NAD 1983
Produced for: National Park Service, Air Resources Division, 2010
Prepared by: E&S Environmental Chemistry

Map N

Figure A

Figure B

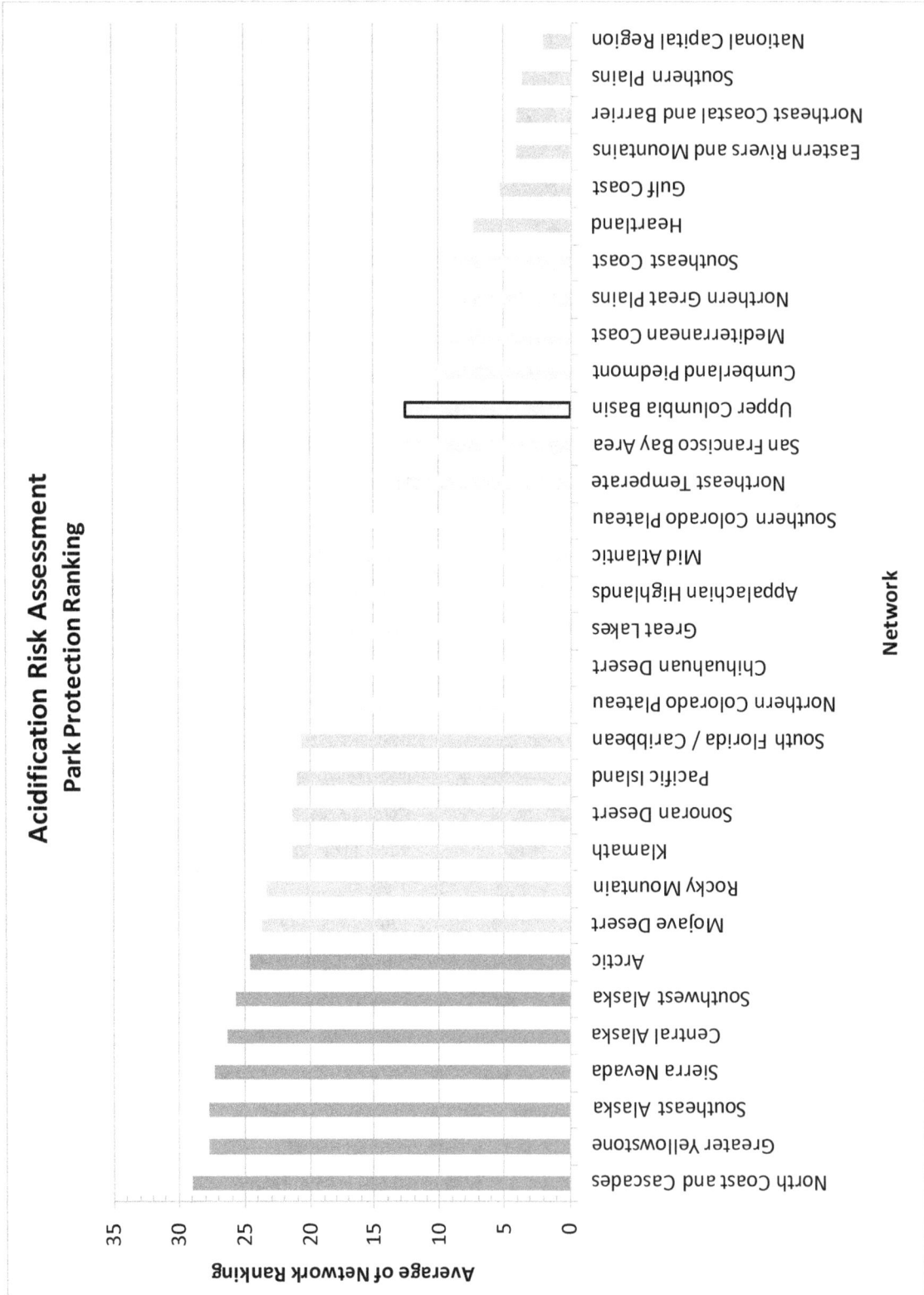

Figure C

Figure D

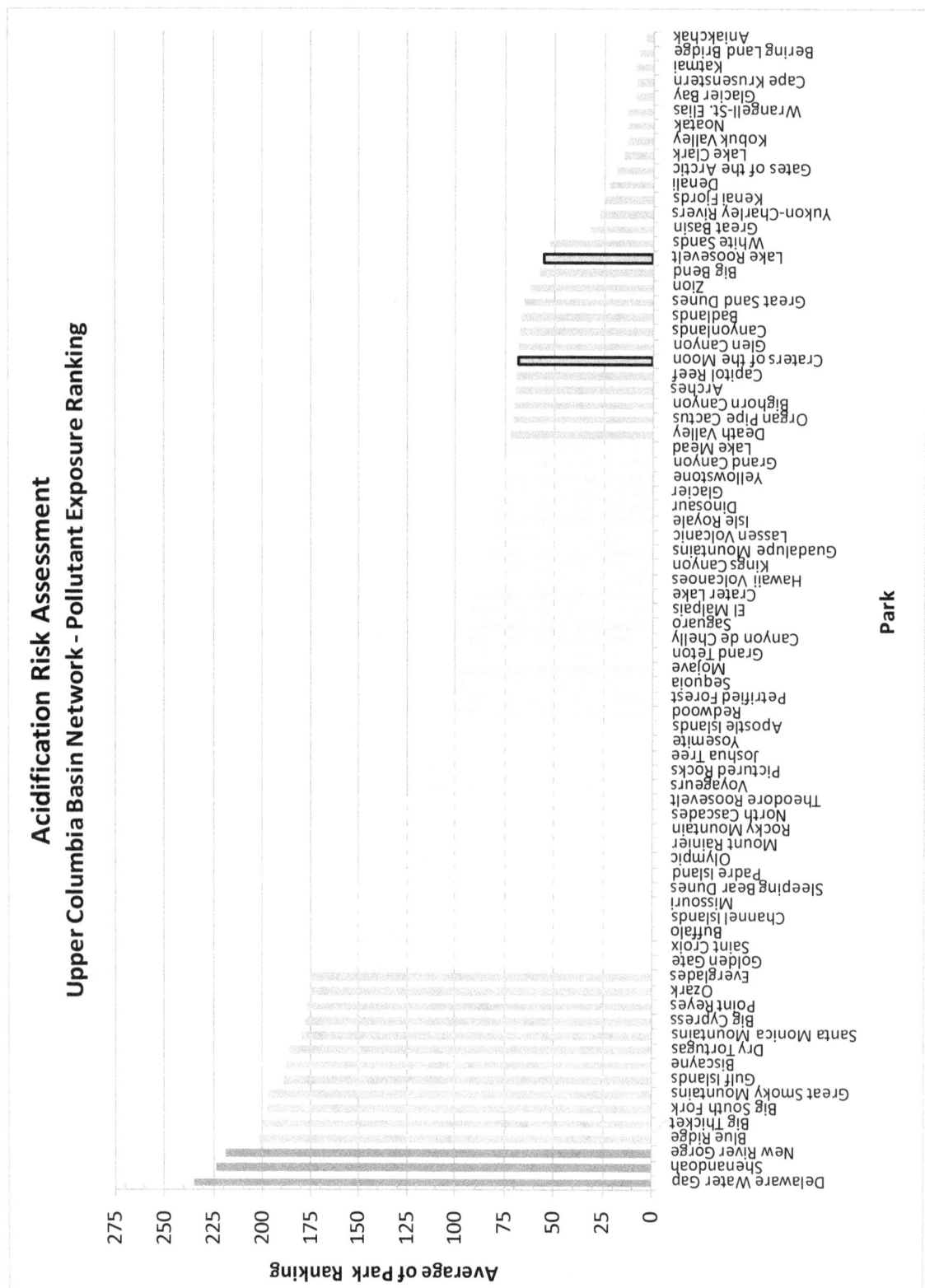

Figure E

Acidification Risk Assessment
Upper Columbia Basin Network - Ecosystem Sensitivity Ranking

Figure F

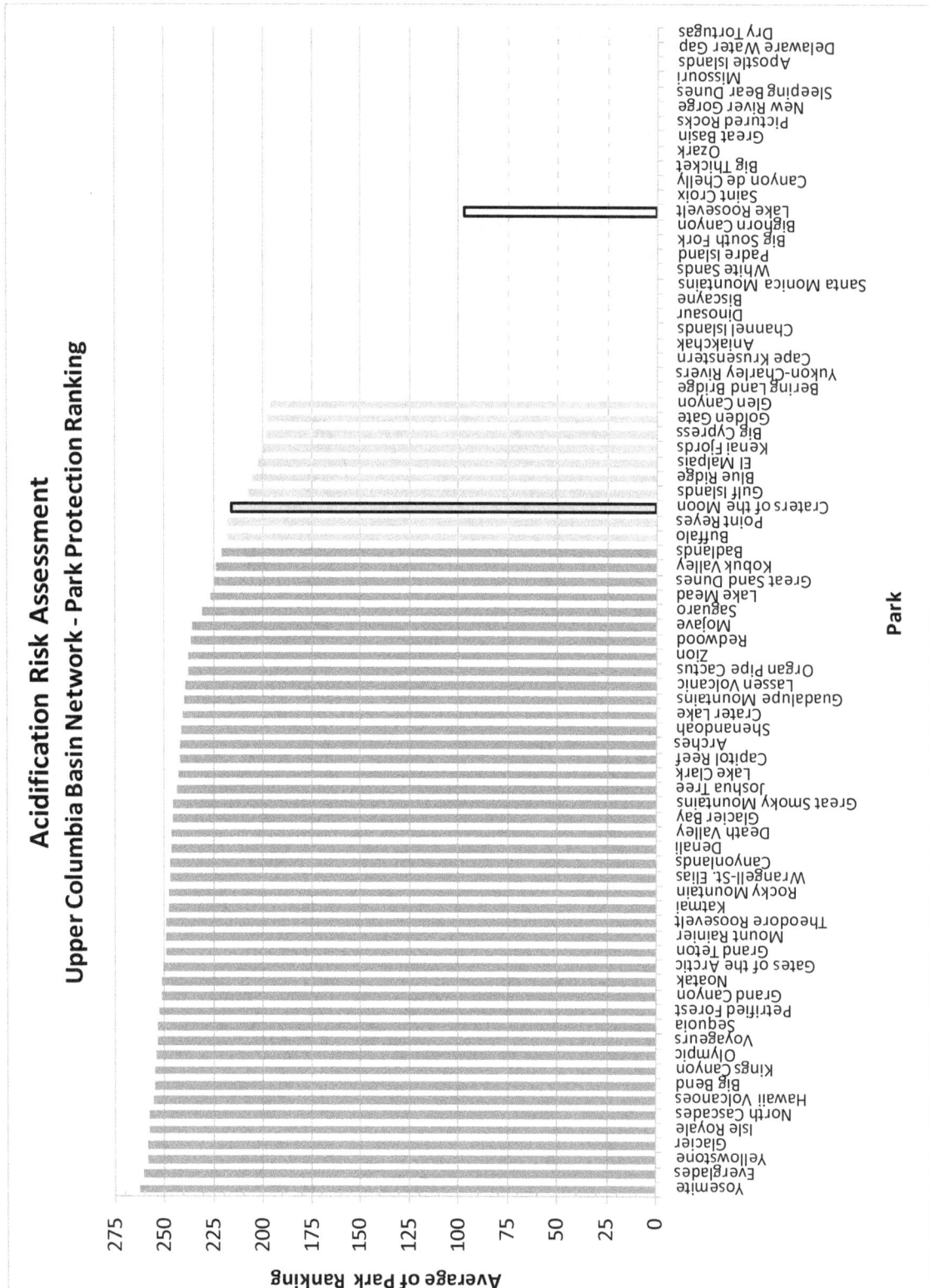

Figure G

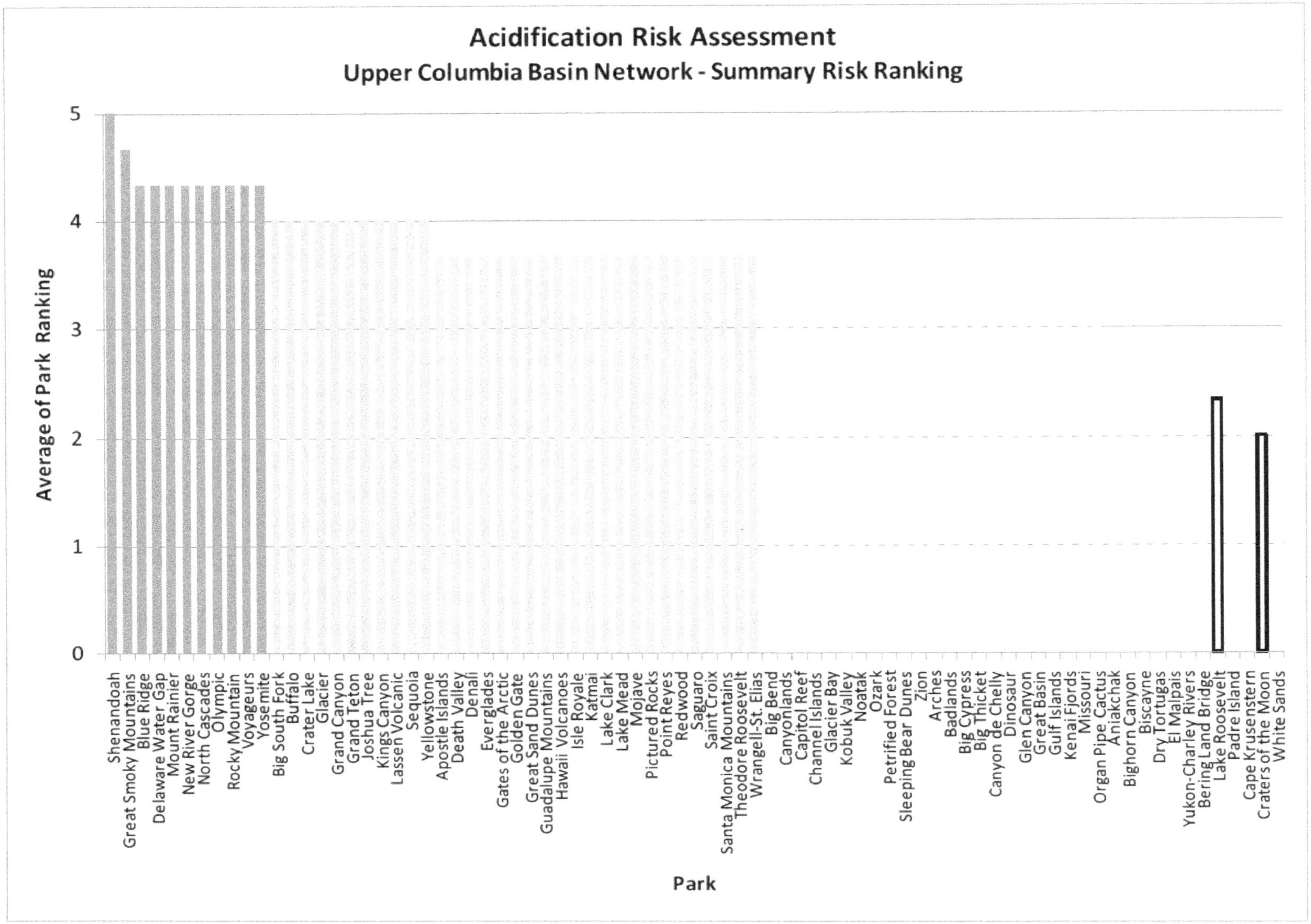

Acidification Risk Assessment
Upper Columbia Basin Network - Summary Risk Ranking
Average of Park Ranking
5
4
3
2
1
0
Shenandoah
Great Smoky Mountains
Blue Ridge
Delaware Water Gap
Mount Rainier
New River Gorge
North Cascades
Olympic
Rocky Mountain
Voyageurs
Yosemite
Big South Fork
Buffalo
Crater Lake
Glacier
Grand Canyon
Grand Teton
Joshua Tree
Kings Canyon
Lassen Volcanic
Sequoia
Yellowstone
Apostle Islands
Death Valley
Denali
Everglades
Gates of the Arctic
Golden Gate
Great Sand Dunes
Guadalupe Mountains
Hawaii Volcanoes
Isle Royale
Katmai
Lake Clark
Lake Mead
Mojave
Pictured Rocks
Point Reyes
Redwood
Saguaro
Saint Croix
Santa Monica Mountains
Theodore Roosevelt
Wrangell-St. Elias
Big Bend
Canyonlands
Capitol Reef
Channel Islands
Glacier Bay
Kobuk Valley
Noatak
Ozark
Petrified Forest
Sleeping Bear Dunes
Zion
Arches
Badlands
Big Cypress
Big Thicket
Canyon de Chelly
Dinosaur
Glen Canyon
Great Basin
Gulf Islands
Kenai Fjords
Missouri
Organ Pipe Cactus
Aniakchak
Bighorn Canyon
Biscayne
Dry Tortugas
El Malpais
Yukon-Charley Rivers
Bering Land Bridge
Lake Roosevelt
Padre Island
Cape Krusenstern
Craters of the Moon
White Sands
Park

Figure H

NPS 963/107420, April 2011